CONTENTS

INTRODUCTION

A county of tall church spires and quaint cottages, often dubbed 'the county of spires and squires', Northamptonshire lies at the heart of England. On the surface it may appear to be a typical English shire, but look more closely and explore its back roads and byways – you will find a wealth of architectural riches and historical heritage. Northamptonshire's churches play a key role in defining the county's character. There is a strong Saxon influence here, and the legacy of the Norman builders is evident too, but it is not just the churches for which Northamptonshire is justly famous. There is no better building material than limestone, and when iron has added a hint of colour to warm the stone, the effect gladdens the eye. Many picturesque small towns and villages in the county make good use of these building materials, and if you embark on a leisurely tour through Northamptonshire, you will see the ironstone evidence virtually everywhere you go.

Many of the towns of Northamptonshire featured in this book were photographed at a time when boot- and shoe-making were still the main industries within the county boundary. The growth in footwear manufacturers in the county in the past was influenced by two natural features – lush grasslands and extensive forests. The bark of oak trees provided the tanning materials, and the flocks and herds grazing on the grassland provided the hides for the leather. For many centuries the Northamptonshire boot- and shoe-making towns teemed with footwear factories and all the trades associated with them: lasts, heels, laces and machinery were also made in workshops.

Northamptonshire covers almost 1,000 square miles of fertile English countryside, stretching from Buckinghamshire and Bedfordshire in the south to Leicestershire and Lincolnshire in the north. Its roots lie deep in the past, and the county has played its part in British history. Roman legions came this way, marching northwards along the ancient routeway known as Watling Street (now the A5), and later the Saxons made their way here from the south. Major battles were fought in the county in both the 15th-century Wars of

the Roses and the 17th-century Civil War. The county's sprawling forests were favoured hunting grounds of Norman kings; here the Council met to enforce the Constitutions of Clarendon, drawn up in 1164 to regulate and monitor the conduct of the clergy, and it was here in central England, too, that the Magna Carta barons met. It was through Northamptonshire that Edward I travelled at the end of the 13th century, escorting his wife Eleanor's body to Westminster Abbey for burial after she died in Nottinghamshire in 1290. He later erected a series of twelve stone crosses along the route to mark the places where the funeral cortege stopped for the night, and two were in Northamptonshire: one at Hardingstone (near Northampton) and the other at Geddington. More than 700 years later, at the close of the 20th century, Northamptonshire once again had a sad role to play in history when the body of Diana, Princess of Wales was taken to the Spencer family home of Althorp to be buried in the grounds of the great house where she spent her childhood.

BLISWORTH, THE GRAND UNION CANAL c1955 B283391

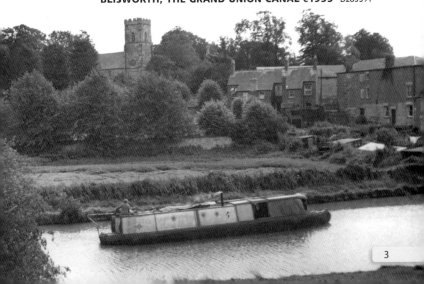

KETTERING, NEWLAND STREET 1922 72235

NORTHAMPTONSHIRE DIALECT WORDS AND PHRASES

'Clang' – to eat voraciously.

'Cack-handed' – left-handed, which came to mean doing something in an awkward fashion.

'Clod Hoppers' – heavy boots.

'Grandad's slippers' – mud on your boots.

'Cod Chops' – used to describe someone whose mouth is permanently open.

'Jitty' – an alley, a narrow walk way between or alongside buildings.

'Peps' – sweets.

'Me dook' - my dear, a term of endearment.

'Chopse' – to chat or chatter.

'Old Frank' – a heron.

'Otch' – move, as in **'Otch up!'** - move up!

'Packup' – a packed lunch.

'Spotting' – starting to rain.

'Knockroad' – awkward.

**NORTHAMPTON, THE DRAPERY
1922** 72174

HAUNTED NORTHAMPTONSHIRE

The Royal Theatre in Northampton is haunted by a 'Grey Lady' who sits in one of the boxes, appears backstage, moves props around and causes the electric system to play up.

A staircase at the Talbot Inn at Oundle (on the left of photograph O103029, opposite) came from Fotheringhay Castle where Mary, Queen of Scots was beheaded in 1587, and it is said that her ghost sometimes descends it.

The shade of 'Captain Slash' haunts the ruined church of St John the Baptist at Boughton. He led a gang that terrorised the district in the early 1800s, demanding protection money from stallholders at the large horse fair that used to be held on Boughton Green. He was eventually captured and hanged at Northampton in 1826.

Charles I is said to have stayed at the Wheatsheaf Inn in Daventry before the defeat of his forces at the battle of Naseby in 1645, where he was visited by the ghost of Lord Strafford, who pleaded with the king not to fight the Parliamentarian army. Charles paid great heed to the warning, but finally followed the advice of his generals to engage the enemy. A similar story is linked with the Wheatsheaf Inn at Northampton.

Northampton has several haunted pubs. Mysterious footsteps have been heard in the Black Lion, where beer barrels are moved around by unseen hands, lights are turned on and off, and there have been sightings of ghostly customers. The Wig and Pen in St Giles Street is said to have a spooky entity in its basement, of which dogs are particularly scared, and the Shipman's is said to be haunted by the ghost of a former manager, Harry Franklin.

The building that is currently occupied by a café at 1a Market Street in Kettering is linked with a ghost story. In the 18th century some soldiers staying in the Dukes Arms, which stood opposite where the café building is now, got into an argument with a drummer boy; he was dragged outside to be murdered in an alleyway, the site of which is now the entrance to the café, and his ghost haunts the building. Several owners of the premises in the 20th century reported feeling uneasy there and noticed mysterious noises, especially from the stock room, and sudden drops in temperature. At one time the staff refused to go the stock room alone, even though they did not know the story. A few years ago a dagger was found in the wall of an upstairs room, but it is not clear whether this was linked with the boy's death.

OUNDLE, NEW STREET c1950 O103029

NORTHAMPTONSHIRE MISCELLANY

After the Norman Conquest the strategic value of Northampton was recognised by the building of a castle, but after the Civil War of the 17th century Charles II took vengeance on the pro-Parliamentarian town by ordering Northampton Castle to be 'slighted' in 1662. Much of the castle survived this treatment, only to succumb in the 19th century when the railway station was built across its site. A plaque commemorates the castle in Chalk Lane, which runs along the course of the castle's eastern moat.

Northampton witnessed many important events in the Middle Ages. The town held both the forerunner of parliament (the royal council) and full parliaments, which in medieval times followed the king around the country. The royal council first met in Northampton from King Stephen's reign (1135-54). The first parliament ever attended by burgesses or merchants, the forerunners of members of the House of Commons, was held at Northampton in 1179. In 1164, in the reign of Henry II, Thomas Becket, the Archbishop of Canterbury, went on trial for treason in Northampton Castle, but escaped from custody and fled to France, before later returning to be murdered in Canterbury Cathedral.

Some of medieval Northampton's monasteries and friaries are recalled in the town's place-names. St Andrew's Priory is commemorated in the names of St Andrew's Street and Priory Street; St James's Abbey is commemorated in the area of Northampton known as St James; and a Franciscan friary is recalled in the name of Greyfriars Street.

NORTHAMPTON, GEORGE ROW 1922 72179

Northampton suffered a great town fire in 1675. Very little survived, apart from the stone churches and the Welsh House in Market Square and Hazelrigg House in Mare Fair. Much of the town's medieval All Saints' Church was destroyed, though the tower and chancel crypt survived. The church was rebuilt in the classical style. The medieval tower was retained, and a forecourt created in front of the portico on the site of the medieval nave. The cupola on the tower was added in 1704, and in 1712 a statue of Charles II was set above the church's portico, in gratitude for the gift of timber from the nearby royal forests that he donated towards the rebuilding of the church after the fire.

Three of Northampton's medieval churches survived the Great Fire of 1675, and two of them, Holy Sepulchre and St Peter's, are of particular interest. Holy Sepulchre has a circular nave whose plan copies that of the Church of the Holy Sepulchre in Jerusalem (photograph 72195, below). Simon de Senlis, Earl of Northampton, had been a crusader and founded this unusual church on his return from the Holy Land, at some time 1100 and 1112. The church was enlarged with a 13th-century chancel and later chapels to its east, and a 14th-century tower and spire added to its west. Equally notable, for its sculptural richness, is St Peter's Church, near the castle site; dating from c1170, it is in the ornate Norman style. The stone carving on the capitals in the church depicts foliage inhabited by mythical winged creatures, writhing figures and animals, and the arches are a profusion of geometric decoration (photograph 72203, opposite). The third surviving medieval church is St Giles, at the east end of town, which has a Norman crossing tower with the rest being later medieval.

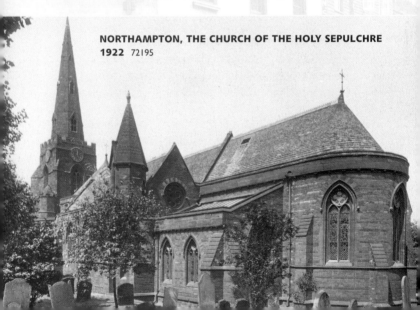

NORTHAMPTON, THE CHURCH OF THE HOLY SEPULCHRE
1922 72195

NORTHAMPTON, ST PETER'S CHURCH, NORMAN ARCH 1922 72203

Abington Park Museum in Northampton occupies a manor house that was originally medieval but was altered in the 17th and 18th centuries. The original house there was the home of William Shakespeare's only surviving grandchild, Elizabeth, who lived there for 20 years with her husband, Sir John Bernard. Shakespeare's direct line came to an end when Elizabeth died, childless, in 1670; she is buried in the nearby church.

By the early 18th century, Northampton was a noted supplier of footwear to the army, as well as to civilians and the American colonies, and the footwear industry remained important throughout the 19th century, but glovemaking was also a prominent local industry in the town in former times. The Drapery was once known as The Glovery, reflecting the importance of the glove-making industry to the town before it was overshadowed by boot- and shoe-making.

The Central Museum and Art Gallery in Northampton holds a fascinating collection of footwear through the ages. Amongst many other items of interest are the shoes that Queen Victoria wore at her wedding in 1840.

Northampton's General Lunatic Asylum on the Billing Road (later named St Andrew's Hospital) was where the rustic labourer poet John Clare ended his days in 1864. Born in 1793 in Helpston, then in Northamptonshire, he was the son of an agricultural labourer, and although he had almost no formal education he began writing poetry from the age of 12. In 1820 Clare's first book, 'Poems Descriptive of Rural Life', was well received, but later volumes failed to sell, and his family fell into poverty. John Clare went insane and spent the last 23 years of his life at Northampton's asylum. He was sometimes referred to as 'the Northamptonshire Peasant Poet', and his poems have remained popular.

NORTHAMPTON, GUILDHALL
1922 72181

Northampton's Guildhall is a heavily decorated Victorian building in St Giles Square (see photograph 72181, above). The exterior features a number of statues representing saints and historical figures, including the Archangel Michael (Northampton's patron saint), Edward IV, Henry VII, Queen Victoria, Edward I, Henry III, Richard I, St George, St Andrew and St Patrick.

Yardley Hastings is a pretty village between Northampton and Bedford. After the Norman Conquest it was held by William the Conqueror's niece. Many centuries later Britain was again facing enemy invasion, and in October 1940 a German parachutist was discovered in the Yardley Hastings area and captured by two local men. When questioned by the police, he was found to be in possession of £100 and a false identity card.

NORTHAMPTON, ABINGTON STREET 1922 72171

ALTHORP PARK, THE HOUSE 1922 72211

Althorp House dates back to the 16th century, when John Spencer, a Warwickshire sheep farmer, acquired the estate and created a park of some 300 acres. Building work on the house began in 1573, and it has been in the ownership of the Spencer family ever since (photograph 72211, above). Althorp was the childhood home of Lady Diana Spencer, who married Charles, Prince of Wales in 1984; as Diana, Princess of Wales, she was laid to rest in on an island in the grounds here after her tragic and untimely death in 1997.

The magnificent house of Castle Ashby is seen in photograph 72221 (below). It was started by the 1st Lord Compton, later the Earl of Northampton, in 1574, originally built to the Elizabethan 'E' plan, and was modified in the 17th century by Inigo Jones, who added the south wing. Running around the whole length of the house on the topmost parapet is a carved inscription in capital letters in Latin, a quotation from Psalm 126 which translates as: 'Unless the Lord build the house, they labour in vain that built it. Unless the Lord keep the house, he watcheth in vain that keepeth it'.

CASTLE ASHBY 1922 72221

BRACKLEY, TOWN HALL c1950 B698010

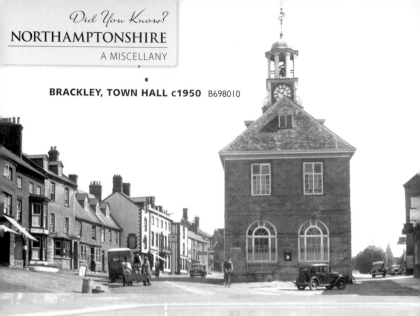

The quaint stone-built town of Brackley was once an important wool centre, and its wide main street is more than a mile long. Brackley's early 18th-century Town Hall was built for the Duke of Bridgewater and is attributed to Sir Christopher Wren.

The Civil War battle of Naseby took place in Northamptonshire in June 1645 when Parliament's New Model Army decisively defeated a Royalist force under Charles I. The battle was one of the most important engagements of the Civil War, the point at which the tide of war turned against Charles I and in favour of Parliament.

Towcester, a small old town on the River Tove, has a number of Georgian houses and an imposing Victorian town hall. The parish church contains a rare 'Treacle Bible', a 1549 edition of the Bible in which the words of Jeremiah 8:22 were translated as 'Is there no tryacle (treacle) in Gilead?'. In those days, 'treacle' was a word for a 'cure-all' as well as a sticky black syrup, but in modern translations the words 'balm' or 'medicine' are used.

North of Daventry, Welton stands on a hillside above the Grand Union Canal. Its name comes from the springs and wells in the area. Inside St Martin's Church in Welton is an ancient tub-shaped font, said to be Saxon, and a small brass recalls that in 1899 five sons of the village carved the splendid pulpit 'for love of the church'. They were also responsible for the alms box, which represents an open hand appealing for coins.

Braunston lies on a hill overlooking the Grand Union Canal, one of Britain's most famous inland waterways, and is a hub of the canal network. Photograph D83014 (below) shows the Welton end of the long Braunston Tunnel, built to connect the Grand Union Canal from London to the Oxford Canal at Braunston. The house over the entrance in the photograph was the home of the tunnel keeper, but has since been demolished. The track up to the left was the route to Braunston for the horses while the narrow boats were 'legged' through the tunnel by the crew, by lying on a plank across the boats and using their feet on the tunnel sides to push the boats through the tunnel.

DAVENTRY, CANAL TUNNEL c1955 D83014

DAVENTRY, MARKET SQUARE c1950 D83008

In the ninth century Daventry was in the Danelaw, the area of England under Danish rule and law. The town's name was recorded as 'Daventre' in the Middle Ages, but this might have been misread from 'Danetre' on a medieval document, when it related to a tree on Borough Hill, the Dane Tree, where the Danes' moot, or court, was held.

In the 12th century the Priory of St Augustine was founded in Daventry, but it was dissolved in 1526. All that survived of the foundation was used as Daventry's parish church until 1752, when it was replaced with the beautiful Holy Cross Parish Church, built in the Palladian style – it is the only Georgian town church in the Peterborough diocese. Designed by William and David Hiorn of Warwick, the design recalls St Martin in the Fields in London, by James Gibb, who later designed All Saints' Church in Derby, now Derby Cathedral. The Hiorn brothers worked as masons at Derby, and when they were approached by Daventry for a new church design, they used Derby as a model.

In the 18th century the old routeway of Watling Street was made into a turnpike road. However, at Weedon the turnpike bore left up Weedon Hill and through Daventry, rejoining Watling Street north of Coventry. The resulting coach traffic, sometimes to 80 coaches a day, brought prosperity to Daventry and many coaching inns were built; most of these are now closed or have been demolished, but two are still in business, both in Brook Street – one is the Dun Cow, and the other is the Saracen's Head.

Dominating photograph D83008 of Daventry (below) are the tall Moot Hall and the Burton Memorial, erected in 1907 in memory of Edmund Charles Burton, 'a staunch churchman, a renowned sportsman and a man greatly beloved'. The Moot Hall was originally a fine Georgian town house which became the residence of the Town Council around 1800, which continued until the re-organisation of local government in the 1970s. Over the years the Moot Hall has also been used for various other purposes, including a women's prison, the mayor's parlour, a museum and TIC and an Indian restaurant.

DAVENTRY, THE BURTON MEMORIAL AND MOOT HALL c1950 D83003

In 1925 the BBC chose Borough Hill near Daventry as the site for their new national radio transmitter, which would bring a 'National' service to everyone in Britain from one site. This was followed in 1932 by the opening of the Empire Station. The masts and aerials on Borough Hill were a feature of the landscape for over 65 years, and Daventry continued to broadcast to the world until 1992, when the facility was transferred to other BBC World Service sites. Many Daventry people reminisce about hearing the General Overseas Service's signature tune, 'Lillibulero', being picked up and transmitted through their electric kettles and toasters!

With rows of charming buildings, Oundle has been described as Northamptonshire's most delightful town. Oundle is famous for its public school, founded by Sir William Laxton in 1556, a prosperous grocer who became Lord Mayor of London. Many of the school's fine stone buildings now dominate the north part of the town. They are mostly Victorian and early 20th century, the majority in Jacobean or Gothic style.

OUNDLE, MARKET PLACE c1950 O103030

OUNDLE, JESUS CHURCH, STOKE HILL c1950 O103026

Jesus Church at Oundle, shown in photograph O103026 (above), was built in 1879 by Arthur Blomfield. It is now a Roman Catholic church. It was designed in the form of a cross, in Gothic style with tall lancet windows in the nave, chancel and transept. The church has an unusual and distinctive central lantern, which starts as a square and then becomes an octagon, with a dome-shaped ceiling.

Near Oundle is the site of the former Fotheringhay Castle, where Mary, Queen of Scots was held prisoner in her final days and where she met her death. She had been kept in 'honourable custody' in England by her cousin Queen Elizabeth I for nearly 20 years whilst Elizabeth decided what to do with her. Eventually Mary became involved in a plot to assassinate Elizabeth and take her throne, and was put on trial for treason in Fotheringhay Castle. She was found guilty, and in February 1587 she was executed in the Great Hall of the castle. The castle fell into disrepair and was demolished in the 17th century. There is now nothing left of it to see except the mound on which it stood.

In Norman and medieval times, Rockingham Forest in Northamptonshire was a royal hunting ground, where nobody could hunt deer or boar, or clear woodland for cultivation, building or other use. There were however advantages in being a Forest village, such as common rights for grazing one's animals, or the right to use any fallen timber.

Rockingham used to be a market town, and the old market cross still stands in the village. Above the village lies a splendid castle. The first castle was a motte and bailey structure built in the time of William the Conqueror, and the first stone castle was founded by his son, William II. The twin-tower gatehouse was added by Henry III in 1270. For 500 years it was used as a royal residence and hunting lodge. In the 19th century Charles Dickens stayed at Rockingham Castle, and wrote part of his novel 'Bleak House' here.

Situated within the remains of Rockingham Forest, the village of Stanion has a 13th-century church with a graceful tower and spire. Inside the church is a bone which, according to legend, is a rib from a cow that provided milk for all the village!

ROCKINGHAM, THE CASTLE c1960 R353009

CORBY, CORPORATION STREET c1965 C337060

The modern industrial town of Corby was once a small Rockingham Forest village with the right to hold a weekly market and two annual fairs. One of the fairs, the Pole Fair, is still held – only every twenty years though, and the last occasion was in 2001. Much modern housing of Corby, especially in the Kingswood and Danesholme areas, is built over Bronze Age, Iron Age and Roman remains, and pottery from the latter era has been found in large quantities. What attracted the Romans, and later the Saxons, were the vast ironstone deposits in the area. Much of the ironstone lay close to the surface, and could easily be extracted by hand or with a minimum of digging. Many old slag heaps are dotted over the area, testimony to the large scale of the industry in the distant past.

Corby's parish church of St John the Baptist is the oldest building in the town, with parts dating to the 12th century. Built of local limestone, it now faces a busy dual carriageway, and stands defiantly against the changes that have affected Corby over the years.

Corby's development took off with the coming of the railway in 1875. During the railway's construction, the vast ironstone deposits of the area were rediscovered. In 1880 a Birmingham industrialist, Samuel Lloyd, investigated the possibility of commercial ironstone quarrying and processing. He amalgamated his company with a Scottish tube-making firm in 1903, and in 1910 Stewarts and Lloyds began commercial production of iron. In 1932 Corby became the site of one of the biggest iron- and steel-making complexes in the world. This was during the Great Depression and swarms of newcomers arrived here looking for employment, many from the north of England and Scotland; thousands of new homes and other facilities had to be built, transforming Corby almost overnight. Photograph C337004 (below) of the Steel Works in the 1950s shows (from left to right) the four blast furnaces, the Brassert towers (gas cleaners), and the cooling towers. A Barclay saddleback engine can be seen on the right, heading in the direction of the tall floodlight in the foreground. The nationalisation of the iron and steel industry in 1967 led to Stewarts & Lloyds becoming part of the British Steel Corporation, but in 1979 the Government decided to close the Steel Works at Corby, to the great dismay of many local people. Everything seen in this photograph has since been demolished, and much of the surrounding area has been redeveloped as a retail park and industrial estate.

CORBY, STEWARTS AND LLOYDS STEEL WORKS c1955 C337004

Kettering originated in pre-Anglo-Saxon England, one of a string of settlements along the River Nene. The name of Kettering in its earliest forms – Cytringan, Kyteringas and Keteiringan – probably means the area was settled by the people of a leader called something like Cuthfrith or Cutfrith, although it could derive from 'cetel', the Saxon word for a narrow valley.

Kettering once had a successful weaving industry. From the 17th century it was a centre for the production of woollen cloth, and later of silk and plush, but by the 19th century it had become an important manufacturing area for boots and shoes, specialising in heavy work boots. From 1850 until 1950 leather was Kettering's business, but cheaper foreign imports began to flood the market, the footwear factories closed, and now only a few businesses in the town are still connected with leather. Kettering also had a significant engineering and clothing industry, and the luxury clothing manufacturers Aquascutum built their first factory here in 1909. Much of the old town centre has been redeveloped, but the market place is still on the site of the first charter market, and the Kettering Heritage Quarter is well worth exploring.

The Fuller Baptist Church in Gold Street in Kettering is named after Andrew Fuller, one of a group of local men who in 1792 founded the Baptist Missionary Society. While Fuller stayed in Kettering and organised the Society, two missionaries from the town set out to make real changes in the world: William Carey went to India, where he translated the Bible into Bengali and founded the Agro-Horticultural Society of India in 1830, and William Knibb went to Kingston, Jamaica, where he was horrified by the realities of slavery and worked for emancipation. After imprisonment he returned to England, where he continued to campaign until the abolition of slavery in the 1830s. He is commemorated in Kettering in the names of Knibb Street and the Knibb Centre.

KETTERING, GOLD STREET 1922 72231

At one time, Kettering was famous for supplying the medical profession with a type of stone that was ground into a powder used to staunch bleeding. This gave the name of Staunch Lane to what is now Lower Street in the town. Many of Kettering's street names have changed over the years. Dryland Street was originally Workhouse Lane, but was renamed after a doctor who had a surgery here. Market Street was formerly Parkstile Lane, and Walker Lane was once known as Pudding Bag Lane because of its cul-de-sac shape. Gold Street was Paul Street in the 18th century, named after two local surgeons, Hugh and Matthew Paul. Meadow Road has had several names, Mill Lane, Gas Street and, before the 19th century, Goose Pasture Lane, because geese were fattened there before being sold at market. A name from the past that is unchanged is Bakehouse Hill, where the original communal town bakehouse stood in the 16th century.

Kettering once had its own small-scale car-making industry: the Robinson car was made for Robinson's garage in Montagu Street. Only three of these cars were constructed, one of which can be seen in the town's Manor House Museum; this car was registered on 1st April 1910, but was built in 1907. It was commissioned by the fourth Dr Roughton to practice in Kettering, and had an extra-large tool box built across the back which held the doctor's medical kit; the box was designed so that it could also be used as an emergency operating table if necessary. The car was 12-horsepower (1884cc), and had a unique cooling system in which the exhaust gases were used to propel fresh air round the engine.

After the First World War, the Kettering industrialist Charles Wicksteed bought 150 acres of land on the edge of town and turned it into Wicksteed Park; it had two boating lakes, and a model railway with two locomotives called 'King Arthur' and 'The Lady of the Lake'. As he grew older, Charles Wicksteed would often visit the park in a two-seater car with his terrier, Jerry, sitting in the passenger seat. In 1927 Jerry disappeared on one of these outings. He was never found, and in his memory his master had a statue erected in the gardens of the park, with the commemorative verse:

> *'Closely bound to a human heart,*
> *Little brown dog, you played your part*
> *In the levelling, building, staying of streams*
> *In the Park that arose from your Master's dreams.'*

Not far from Kettering is the pretty village of Barton Seagrave. Northamptonshire's most famous historian, John Bridges, was born at Barton Seagrave Hall in 1666.

Islip is a picturesque village on the western bank of the River Nene, between Kettering and Thrapston. At one time, Islip House in the village was the home of Thomas Squire, who was instrumental in making the River Nene navigable between Peterborough and Thrapston. The river was eventually opened to craft in 1737.

KETTERING, PARISH
CHURCH & MEMORIAL
CROSS 1922 72239

The superb Perpendicular west tower of Kettering's parish church is 179ft high, with a battlemented spire (see photograph 72239, opposite). There are four stages, with the upper (bell) stage having three openings. The church's peal of twelve bells is one of the largest in the country. Three of the bells were cast by Thomas Eayre (1691-1757), a member of the well-known family of Kettering bellfounders which is commemorated in the name of Belfry Lane in the town, off Wadcroft, formerly Bellfounders Lane.

Inside Kettering's parish church of St Peter and St Paul are some medieval wall paintings, including some faded relics of coloured angels, but the church also holds a memorial of the Second World War from when the United States Airforce had a base at nearby Grafton Underwood. On their return from forays over Germany, the US pilots used the spire of Kettering's parish church as a landmark on their way home. A statue of St Christopher, patron saint of travellers, was a gift to the church after the war from the men of the 384th Zebra (NCO) and Officers Clubs, who also gave a statue of St Christopher to the town's Roman Catholic church of St Edward.

Kettering's art gallery was named after a noted local artist, Sir Alfred East, and was built to house a collection of paintings that he left to the town. At the end of the 19th century Sir Alfred East was an establishment artist, an associate of the Royal Academy and President of the Royal Society of British Artists. He spent summers in Cornwall, often visiting another famous Kettering painter, Thomas Cooper Gotch, who lived and worked in Newlyn. Their loose vigorous paintings in sunlit colours attempted to bring the brilliance of French Impressionism into England.

THRAPSTON, HIGH STREET 1951 T104008

On the road to Thrapston from Finedon is the Wellington Tower, a round tower built by General Arbuthnot, a friend of the Duke of Wellington. Whilst staying with General Arbuthnot, the Duke commented on the similarity of the local landscape to that of the battlefield of Waterloo in Belgium, and the General built the tower around 1820 to commemorate the victory at Waterloo in 1815 over Napoleon's forces.

The village of Rushton is famous for its connections with the Tresham family of nearby Rushton Hall. Francis Tresham, described as 'a wild and unstayed man', was the son of Sir Thomas Tresham who built the Triangular Lodge seen on page 49, and was one of the conspirators of the Gunpowder Plot to blow up the House of Lords during the State Opening of Parliament in November 1605, and thus assassinate James I. After the plot was discovered he was arrested, and later died in prison.

Desborough is a small town on the road to Market Harborough. Long ago there was a Saxon settlement here; three huge stones were discovered in the rectory garden, the largest covered on two sides with Saxon lettering. A Saxon mirror and necklace that were also found here were given to the British Museum. In the village centre is the Desborough Cross: it looks like a giant gatepost, and according to some sources, the cross was indeed once part of the entrance to a local country estate.

Photograph 72253 on pages 36-37 of Geddington shows the famous stone cross at the village centre, one of a number of 'Eleanor Crosses' which were built to commemorate Eleanor of Castile, the beloved wife of Edward I who died in 1290 whilst she and the king were at Harby in Nottinghamshire. Her body was taken from there to London for burial in Westminster Abbey, and the king later had twelve commemorative crosses built at the places along the route where her funeral cortège rested for the night. Only three of the original crosses remain – the other two are at Hardingstone near Northampton (although damaged, it remains an important landmark on the London road), and Waltham Cross in Hertfordshire – and Geddington's is the best preserved, standing as a sad commemoration of a royal love story. The cross contains a number of small statues of the queen, who was probably 13 when she married Edward, and bore him a total of 16 children.

There was once a royal hunting palace near Geddington, but nothing remains of it now apart from some fragments in the village church of St Mary Magadalene, seen on the right of photograph 72253 (page 37), distinguished by its tower and octagonal spire.

Pronounced 'Rowell', the town of Rothwell possibly takes its name from an old Danish word meaning 'red well'. By the Middle Ages it had become a town of some importance; a market charter was granted by King John in 1204, as well as permission for an annual fair which is still held here during the week following Trinity Sunday. Rothwell's most famous landmark, the old Market House in the town centre, was built by a local lord of the manor, Thomas Tresham. Work began in 1577, but the building remained unfinished until 1895 when J A Gotch, a Northamptonshire architect, roofed it and filled in the arches. It was originally known as Rothwell Cross, and acquired its present name much later. On the central frieze is a Latin inscription dedicating the building to the town and country, and on the upper frieze are 90 coats-of-arms of landed Northamptonshire families. The building is used today as council offices.

**ROTHWELL, THE MARKET HOUSE
1922** 72249

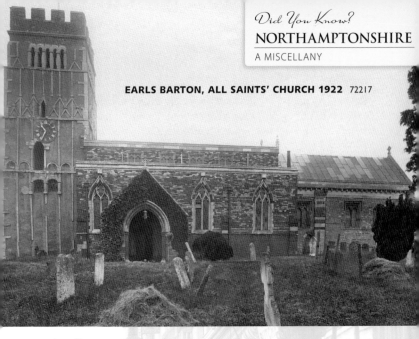

EARLS BARTON, ALL SAINTS' CHURCH 1922 72217

Rothwell's ironstone Holy Trinity Church is the longest church in the county. Inside the church, a gruesome sight greets visitors who descend into the vaulted 13th-century crypt. The crypt had been sealed up for years; when it was rediscovered and opened, it was found to contain thousands of bones and skulls collected from an old churchyard. They remain there, neatly stacked. The crypt at Rothwell is one of only two surviving (filled) bone crypts, or ossuaries, in England and is open once a week to the public.

The name of the village of Earls Barton reflects its ancient origins: in former times the Earl of Huntingdon lived nearby, providing the 'Earl' part of the name, and the village gets the other half of its name from his association with barley farming – the village is surrounded by the fertile countryside of the Nene valley. Earls Barton also boasts a richly decorated Saxon tower to its church of All Saints, where the strip-like stonework was probably intended to resemble timberwork; a remarkable survival, the church is one of England's most important Anglo-Saxon monuments (see photograph 72217, above).

Rushden, a town originally noted for lace making, grew greatly in the 19th century as houses were built for the boot and shoe workers who were needed to service about 100 shoe factories that used to be there. Rushden has a superb medieval church in its higher churchyard to the south of the High Street, its dominance emphasised by a tall tower and crocket-fringed spire, a fine example of Perpendicular Gothic.

Close to the county boundary with Buckinghamshire and Bedfordshire is the village of Bozeat, which was at the heart of a thriving weaving industry 600 years ago; the Weavers' Guild donated a rich assortment of gifts to the parish church. Later, Bozeat became a centre for footwear production, and many soldiers in the First World War marched off to battle wearing locally-made boots.

RUSHDEN, HIGH STREET AND POST OFFICE
c1890 R223316

STANWICK, PARISH CHURCH c1960
S628002

The parish church of St Lawrence in the centre of the village of Stanwick has a most unusual 13th-century octagonal tower, surmounted by the more usual octagonal spire, reaching a total height of 155 feet.

Wellingborough, an ancient market town, grew up at the crossroads of two major routes. It was granted to Croyland Abbey in Lincolnshire in AD948, and continued to be owned by the abbey until it was dissolved under Henry VIII in 1539. Remnants of the monks' grange house are buried within the present Croyland Hall, while their tithe barn has survived nearby and has been well restored. Mentioned in the Domesday Book of 1086, and briefly a spa town in the 17th century, Wellingborough was granted market rights by King John in 1201. Wellingborough developed rapidly in the second half of the 20th century, when it became a London overspill town. The growth of the town has entailed much redevelopment, but the past is still very much present in the town's plan and architecture. The Hind Hotel in Sheep Street (photograph W279050, below) is one of the town's best surviving older buildings and a former coaching inn. It dates from the 1640s and is built in the local russet ironstone with limestone dressings; its central carriageway was blocked and the timber porch built around 1900. Oliver Cromwell is said to have stayed at the Hind in 1645, en route to the battle of Naseby.

WELLINGBOROUGH, THE HIND HOTEL AND SHEEP STREET c1955 W279050

WELLINGBOROUGH, MIDLAND ROAD 1949 W279025

Midland Road in Wellingborough was formed in the early 1860s after the Midland Railway station opened east of the town centre, and the end nearer Market Street became one of the town's busiest shopping streets. Nowadays, you would not recognise the road as the same place as that seen in photograph W279025 (above), for the development of the Swansgate Shopping Centre resulted in all the buildings on the left side of the road being replaced by the shopping mall's side elevation, but the Old King's Arms in Market Street, closing the vista up Midland Road, survives. Built in Queen Anne style around 1890, it was converted by the 1970s to shops.

Wellingborough has an architectural masterpiece within its boundaries: Sir Ninian Comper's incomparable St Mary's Church at the junction of Knox Road and Elsdon Road, started in 1906 but not completed until 1968. The interior of this grand ironstone and limestone church is quite outstanding. Comper was one of the country's finest church architects of the last century, and this church is a real jewel in the town's crown.

All Saints' Church in Wellingborough boasts stained-glass windows by a famous 19th-century designer, Charles Eamer Kempe, who also designed the alabaster altarpiece and the oak panels in the chancel. All Hallows' Church in the town also has some outstanding stained-glass windows, in this case from a number of famous contemporary artists including Evie Hone, John Piper and Patrick Reyntiens. Inside the church are also some older stained-glass window panels in the north aisle, depicting a man riding upon a bear. This is a reference to an incident during the 17th century. The town's Royalist vicar, Thomas Jones, was arrested for defying Puritan soldiers and taken to Northampton Gaol; the story goes that he was forced to ride part of the way on the town's performing bear.

WELLINGBOROUGH, ALL HALLOWS PARISH CHURCH 1954 W279051

SPORTING NORTHAMPTONSHIRE

A monument to Lieutenant-Colonel Edgar Mobbs, who was killed in the First World War, stands in Abington Square in Northampton (photograph 72168, page 46). Mobbs was a noted Midlands sportsman, and the monument depicts sporting as well as battle scenes. He was captain of Northampton (Rugby) Football Club from 1907 to 1913, and played seven times for England. He is commemorated each year by the Mobbs Memorial Match between East Midlands and the Barbarians, preceded by a wreath-laying ceremony at the memorial. Proceeds from the match go towards the Mobbs Memorial Fund, which assists East Midlands rugby clubs with youth development.

Northampton Town Football Club, 'The Cobblers', had an extraordinary decade in the 1960, rising from Division Four in 1961 to Division One, only to fall all the way back down by 1969 after spending a solitary season in the top flight, during which Northampton did the 'double' over Aston Villa, winning at home and away; the clubs have never met in another League match, so the Cobblers have a 100% win record over one of the country's most famous clubs! A former player with Northampton Town was the entertainer Des O'Connor; he was evacuated to Northampton during the Second World War, and was a professional on Town's books for a while.

Northamptonshire County Cricket Club plays most of its games at the county ground in Northampton, which staged the first women's test match between England and Australia in 1931. The nickname for the county club of 'The Steelbacks' derives from a name given to the men of the Northamptonshire Regiment who were famous for their grit and tough resolve in adversity, qualities which the county players strive to emulate.

About four miles from Towcester is the Silverstone motor racing circuit, currently the home of the British Grand Prix, which the ground first hosted in 1948. Half the ground is in Northamptonshire, and the other half in Buckinghamshire. The circuit was built on the site of a former bomber base of the Second World War, RAF Silverstone.

**NORTHAMPTON
MARKET PLACE &
MOBBS MEMORIAL
1922** 72168

Northamptonshire has a proud rugby tradition. The Northampton Saints (the club's original name was Northampton St James) were European champions in 2000, defeating Munster to win the Heineken Club. Another notable club is Kettering Rugby Club; a significant name in the club's history is Ralph Bainbridge, who spent five years as club captain, during which time the team had a run of 52 games unbeaten.

Wellingborough Town Football Club was originally formed in 1867, making it the oldest football club in Northamptonshire and the sixth oldest football club in the country, although the club was reformed under the same name in 2004, after the previous club of that name folded in 2002. Wellingborough Town has a place in football history because in 1879 it was the first football club to play under floodlights, at the Bassett's Close ground. The club's nickname is 'The Doughboys', thought to derive from a local speciality dish of a hock of bacon cooked with onions and carrots in a pastry case, known as Ock 'n' Dough.

Kettering Town Football Club, founded in 1872, has had a number of well-known managers, two in particular being Ron Atkinson and Derek Dougan. Ron Atkinson, manager from 1971-74, led the Poppies to two consecutive promotions before going on to manage a string of big League clubs. Derek Dougan, a former Wolves striker, was notable for a pioneering attempt to introduce shirt advertising to the English game: in January 1976 Kettering took to the field in shirts showing the name of Kettering Tyres. This led to an FA fine and Town were forced to remove the name, yet within a few years the FA was to allow shirt advertising. Kettering has a place in football history, as Scott Endersby became the youngest ever player to play in an FA Cup match when he turned out for the Poppies against Tilbury on 26 November 1977, at the age of 15.

Towcester is famous for its racecourse, one of the most scenically attractive in the country and sited in beautiful parkland, and many important National Hunt horseracing events are held there. Races here can result in some exciting finishes, as the final gallop to the winning post is run uphill, testing the horses' stamina to the limit.

QUIZ QUESTIONS

Answers on page 52.

1. Which fine country house in Northamptonshire is so impressive in its magnificence that it has been described as 'the English Versailles'?

2. Which well-known high street chain of shoe shops from the not-so-distant past was based in Kettering?

3. One of England's most unusual buildings is the Triangular Lodge at Rushton, a few miles from Kettering (see photograph R272010, opposite). Although it looks like a folly, it was actually designed to be a symbol of …what?

4. Northamptonshire is famous for its boot- and shoe-making heritage, but whereabouts in the county can you find a boot that was specially made for an elephant?

5. What is the link between Northamptonshire and George Washington, first President of the United States of America?

6. What is the link between Northampton and a unique political assassination in British history?

7. Daventry was an important town on the coaching routes in the past, and was famous for the manufacture of which items linked with this business?

8. Here is a nostalgic one for drivers of a certain age – what is unusual about the 'No Waiting' sign seen on the right hand side of photograph W279025 on page 43 of Midland Road in Wellingborough?

Directions for being a Genius!

Read directions on game. Each time tee is jumped remove it.
Leaving hole #1 empty; begin with #4 jumping #2.

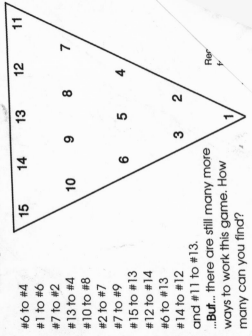

#6 to #4
#1 to #6
#7 to #2
#13 to #4
#10 to #8
#2 to #7
#7 to #9
#15 to #13
#12 to #14
#6 to #13
#14 to #12
and #11 to #13.

...**But**... there are still many more
ways to work this game. How
many can you find?

Qualls & Son Novelties, Inc.
Lebanon, TN 37087

9. What is the link between Northamptonshire and Wellington boots?

10. What is the significance of the acronym PLUTO to Corby's history?

RUSHTON, TRIANGULAR LODGE c1955 R272010

RECIPE

FEAST PLUM PUDDING

This is a recipe from Northamptonshire, where it was originally cooked in the baker's oven after the day's baking had been completed, and left all night to cook in the cooling oven. It is a good way of using up stale bread.

> 350g/12oz stale white bread, without crusts
> 115g/4oz raisins, or chopped dates
> 115g/4oz currants
> 25g/1oz mixed peel
> 50g/2oz sugar
> 1 egg
> 115g/4oz shredded suet
> ¼ teaspoonful grated nutmeg

Pre-heat the oven to 180°C/350°F/Gas Mark 4.

Cut the bread into cubes, and soak in water for 10 minutes, then squeeze out the moisture and mix it with the other ingredients.

Put the mixture into a well-greased ovenproof dish, and cover with foil. Cook in the pre-heated oven for half an hour, then reduce the heat to 140°C/275°F/Gas Mark 1½ and cook for a further 2 hours. If required, the pudding can be left in the oven for a little longer with the heat turned off.

Feast Plum Pudding can be re-heated before serving, but was usually eaten cold.

RECIPE

NORTHAMPTONSHIRE CHEESECAKES

Small cheesecakes were traditionally made in Northamptonshire to be eaten at sheep-shearing time.

> 225g/8oz shortcrust pastry
> 175g/6oz curd cheese, or cream cheese
> 50g/2oz butter or margarine
> 2 eggs, beaten
> 75g/3oz caster sugar
> 115g/4oz currants
> Finely grated rind of 1 lemon
> ¼ teaspoonful almond extract
> ½ teaspoonful ground nutmeg

Pre-heat the oven to 180°C/350°F/Gas Mark 4.

Roll out the pastry on a lightly floured surface, and use it to line 14-16 lightly greased patty tins.

In a bowl, beat the curd or cream cheese until it is smooth. Put the butter or margarine into a saucepan with the sugar and beaten eggs and heat gently, stirring all the time, until the mixture has thickened – be careful not to allow it to boil. Remove the pan from the heat, and stir in the curd or cream cheese, the currants, lemon rind and almond essence, making sure that the ingredients are well combined.

Fill the patty tins with the mixture, dust the cheesecakes with a little ground nutmeg and bake for 20-25 minutes until well risen. Serve hot or cold.

QUIZ ANSWERS

1. Boughton House near Geddington is so magnificent that it has been described as the 'English Versailles' (see photograph G84023, opposite). Built around the theme of time, with seven courtyards, 52 chimney stacks and 365 windows, Boughton House was begun in 1530 by Sir Edward Montagu. The house was extended several times, culminating in the building of the north front in the late 17th century. It was the home of the first Duke of Montagu, who held the post of Ambassador to the Court of Louis XIV and brought back with him an impressive collection of French furniture and china.

2. A well-known high street chain of shoe shops in past years was Timpsons Shoes; the company had branches all over Britain, but the shoes were made in Kettering. Its founder, William Timpson, went to work at the age of eleven in a shoe shop in Manchester; he noticed that his Lancashire customers had wider-than-average feet, so when he later returned to Kettering he started a shoe-making workshop in an old silk-weaving mill in Market Street to make wide fittings for the northern market. Timpsons was so successful that in 1921 one of the most modern factories in Britain, a huge glass structure like the Crystal Palace, was built on the edge of Kettering. By the 1950s Timpsons was supplying 22,000 pairs of shoes a week for 262 retail shops, but gradually demand for British-made footwear decreased, and Timpsons sold its great glass factory in 1972.

3. The Triangular Lodge was built by Sir Thomas Tresham of Rushton Hall in 1593. It was officially erected as a rabbit warrener's lodge, but was actually a secret reflection of Tresham's Roman Catholic faith in a zealously Protestant era, after his release from a long imprisonment for being a 'Papist'. This stone manifestation of Tresham's Catholicism takes its name from the fact that everything about it is triangular, making it an emblem of the Holy Trinity; it is constructed according to a factor of three, with three sides, three floors, three windows on each floor, and three gables.

4. In the Northampton Museum and Art Gallery is a huge boot which was worn by an elephant in 1959 when the British Alpine Expedition re-enacted Hannibal's crossing of the Alps with his army and battle elephants to attack Rome in 218BC.

5. George Washington, the first President of the United States of America, was a direct descendant of Lawrence Washington, who was twice Mayor of Northampton. Lawrence Washington bought Sulgrave Manor near Northampton from Henry VIII at the Dissolution in the 1530s; it remained in the family until 1610. It was Lawrence Washington's son John who emigrated to America and became the great-grandfather of George Washington.

Sulgrave Manor is now a museum, much visited by American tourists. The Washington coat-of-arms, which can be seen above the porch of Sulgrave Manor, is thought to have inspired the design of the Star and Stripes, the flag of the USA.

6. The only Prime Minister in British history to have been assassinated was Spencer Perceval, who was shot in the lobby of the House of Commons by John Bellingham in 1812. Spencer Perceval was also Northampton's MP.

7. Daventry's importance as a centre for the coaching trade gave rise to a lucrative trade in making whips for the coachmen, a result of Northamptonshire's long association with leather which also developed the county's boot- and shoe-making industry.

8. The 'No Waiting' sign seen in photograph W279025 (page 43) was used during the 'unilateral waiting' period in the late 1940s and 50s, when vehicles could wait on one side of the road on odd days of the month and on the opposite side on even days. The signs were hinged in half moons so that they could be tipped over to show which side of the road was currently available for parking.

9. The first Wellington boots were made for the Duke of Wellington in the village of Stanwick in Northamptonshire by one of its local boot-making businesses, a fact recalled in the name of the Duke of Wellington pub in Church Street in the village.

10. The acronym PLUTO is a reminder of a significant part played by the former Steel Works at Corby in the war effort during the Second World War. PLUTO is formed from the initial letters of 'Pipe Line Under The Ocean', the codename for the production of miles of steel tubing at Corby which was used for conveying fuel across the English Channel to the Allies in Europe, following the D-Day landings in 1944.

GEDDINGTON, BOUGHTON HOUSE c1955   G84023

FRANCIS FRITH

PIONEER VICTORIAN PHOTOGRAPHER

Francis Frith, founder of the world-famous photographic archive, was a complex and multi-talented man. A devout Quaker and a highly successful Victorian businessman, he was philosophical by nature and pioneering in outlook. By 1855 he had already established a wholesale grocery business in Liverpool, and sold it for the astonishing sum of £200,000, which is the equivalent today of over £15,000,000. Now in his thirties, and captivated by the new science of photography, Frith set out on a series of pioneering journeys up the Nile and to the Near East.

INTRIGUE AND EXPLORATION

He was the first photographer to venture beyond the sixth cataract of the Nile. Africa was still the mysterious 'Dark Continent', and Stanley and Livingstone's historic meeting was a decade into the future. The conditions for picture taking confound belief. He laboured for hours in his wicker dark-room in the sweltering heat of the desert, while the volatile chemicals fizzed dangerously in their trays. Back in London he exhibited his photographs and was 'rapturously cheered' by members of the Royal Society. His reputation as a photographer was made overnight.

VENTURE OF A LIFE-TIME

By the 1870s the railways had threaded their way across the country, and Bank Holidays and half-day Saturdays had been made obligatory by Act of Parliament. All of a sudden the working man and his family were able to enjoy days out, take holidays, and see a little more of the world.

With typical business acumen, Francis Frith foresaw that these new tourists would enjoy having souvenirs to commemorate their days out. For the next thirty years he travelled the country by train and by pony and trap, producing fine photographs of seaside resorts and beauty spots that were keenly bought by millions of Victorians. These prints were painstakingly pasted into family albums and pored over during the dark nights of winter, rekindling precious memories of summer excursions. Frith's studio was soon supplying retail shops all over the country, and by 1890 F Frith & Co had become the greatest specialist photographic publishing company in the world, with over 2,000 sales outlets, and pioneered the picture postcard.

FRANCIS FRITH'S LEGACY

Francis Frith had died in 1898 at his villa in Cannes, his great project still growing. By 1970 the archive he created contained over a third of a million pictures showing 7,000 British towns and villages.

Frith's legacy to us today is of immense significance and value, for the magnificent archive of evocative photographs he created provides a unique record of change in the cities, towns and villages throughout Britain over a century and more. Frith and his fellow studio photographers revisited locations many times down the years to update their views, compiling for us an enthralling and colourful pageant of British life and character.

We are fortunate that Frith was dedicated to recording the minutiae of everyday life. For it is this sheer wealth of visual data, the painstaking chronicle of changes in dress, transport, street layouts, buildings, housing and landscape that captivates us so much today, offering us a powerful link with the past and with the lives of our ancestors.

Computers have now made it possible for Frith's many thousands of images to be accessed almost instantly. The archive offers every one of us an opportunity to examine the places where we and our families have lived and worked down the years. Its images, depicting our shared past, are now bringing pleasure and enlightenment to millions around the world a century and more after his death.

For further information visit: www.francisfrith.com

INTERIOR DECORATION

Frith's photographs can be seen framed and as giant wall murals in thousands of pubs, restaurants, hotels, banks, retail stores and other public buildings throughout Britain. These provide interesting and attractive décor, generating strong local interest and acting as a powerful reminder of gentler days in our increasingly busy and frenetic world.

FRITH PRODUCTS

All Frith photographs are available as prints and posters in a variety of different sizes and styles. In the UK we also offer a range of other gift and stationery products illustrated with Frith photographs, although many of these are not available for delivery outside the UK – see our web site for more information on the products available for delivery in your country.

THE INTERNET

Over 100,000 photographs of Britain can be viewed and purchased on the Frith web site. The web site also includes memories and reminiscences contributed by our customers, who have personal knowledge of localities and of the people and properties depicted in Frith photographs. If you wish to learn more about a specific town or village you may find these reminiscences fascinating to browse. Why not add your own comments if you think they would be of interest to others? See **www.francisfrith.com**

PLEASE HELP US BRING FRITH'S PHOTOGRAPHS TO LIFE

Our authors do their best to recount the history of the places they write about. They give insights into how particular towns and villages developed, they describe the architecture of streets and buildings, and they discuss the lives of famous people who lived there. But however knowledgeable our authors are, the story they tell is necessarily incomplete.

Frith's photographs are so much more than plain historical documents. They are living proofs of the flow of human life down the generations. They show real people at real moments in history; and each of those people is the son or daughter of someone, the brother or sister, aunt or uncle, grandfather or grandmother of someone else. All of them lived, worked and played in the streets depicted in Frith's photographs.

We would be grateful if you would give us your insights into the places shown in our photographs: the streets and buildings, the shops, businesses and industries. Post your memories of life in those streets on the Frith website: what it was like growing up there, who ran the local shop and what shopping was like years ago; if your workplace is shown tell us about your working day and what the building is used for now. Read other visitors' memories and reconnect with your shared local history and heritage. With your help more and more Frith photographs can be brought to life, and vital memories preserved for posterity, and for the benefit of historians in the future.

Wherever possible, we will try to include some of your comments in future editions of our books. Moreover, if you spot errors in dates, titles or other facts, please let us know, because our archive records are not always completely accurate—they rely on 140 years of human endeavour and hand-compiled records. You can email us using the contact form on the website.

Thank you!

For further information, trade, or author enquiries
please contact us at the address below:

**The Francis Frith Collection, 6 Oakley Business Park,
Wylye Road, Dinton, Wiltshire SP3 5EU England.**
Tel: +44 (0)1722 716 376 Fax: +44 (0)1722 716 881
e-mail: sales@francisfrith.co.uk **www.francisfrith.com**